The Poet's Heart

Poems of Faith

By Debra G. Price

ISBN: 978-1-257-13365-9

Usurper

Myself, the usurper,

I sit on the throne

Demanding my wants

In imperative tone.

Himself, the Almighty,

Should rule in my heart,

But I leave Him chained

In a very small part.

If I give a command,

Or I write a decree,

It is never fulfilled

(it depends upon me).

I never make progress;

I mess up each task;

I can't meet my needs,

And my smile is a mask.

My Lord, in the dungeon,

Has paid all the cost

To give me sweet peace,

And the joy I have lost.

Myself, the usurper,

In misery cry,

For help and relief

To the One I deny.

I could have such rest,

If I yield Him control,

But His hands are tied

In that dark dismal hole.

When I lay down the scepter

And pick up my cross;

When I humble myself

And count all gain as loss:

Himself, the Almighty,

From that lowly den,

Comes back to His throne

And forgives me again...

And again...

And again...

By Debra G. Price

The "I AM"

When I ask who He is,

He says, "I Am"

Eternal, immutable God

With all power and wisdom;

Father, Spirit, and Son

Always everywhere;

The only One.

When I ask for something special,

He says, "I Am"

Ever above and beyond all;

The Best, the Greatest, the Most;

Surpassing description;

Precious, Wonderful;

The matchless One.

When I ask for something more,

He says, "I Am"

Enough, without these earthly things;

Sufficient for all your need;

I give satisfaction;

Lasting, tangible;

The complete One.

When I ask for my heart's desire,

He says, "I Am"

Everything you are hoping for

Is found in my best for you.

When all has been done;

Loving and giving;

The perfect One.

By Debra G. Price

Music for Eternity

A simple tune

An imperfect melody

Is all I have to bring my praise

And so I sing

This little shadow song

Until the day when I get home

Imagine this:

A Heavenly choir

Saints and angels in harmony

All points of praise

In counter melodies

And ancient stars will lead the way

Irresistible melodies

With intricate harmonies

Rhythms that move us

In perfect praise

So I'm still longing for the music of the ages

Celestial songs to sing for all eternity

Pouring out of Ivory Palaces

Along the golden streets

Sweeping all across the universe

Praising Christ my Lord and King

But now I sing

My simple melody

With imperfect harmony

Because my praise can't wait.

By Debra G. Price

Don't Let This Moment Pass

This little child

Who holds your hand

Is looking in your eyes

And hopes you understand

You hold his heart

Don't turn away

Explain the truth of Christ

Before another day

When wonder dies

And hearts turn cold

It's hard to share what matters

When the child is growing old

Time travels fast

And slips away

Don't wait to speak the truth

Soon it will be too late

Don't let this moment pass

To reach the children

Their hearts are tender now

And filled with wonder

They want to know what's true

The Gospel someone shared with you

Don't let this moment pass them by

Can you hear the Savior cry?

Feed my Lambs

By Debra G. Price

Too Small

Sometimes I stumble in the darkness of confusion

My focus fixed on ordinary dreams

I'm blinded to the path that I should follow

Where God has planned extraordinary things

And I ask Him, Lord, is this too much to ask for?

Is this dream beyond what reason should require?

Have I built my hopes too high?

Perhaps my faith is just too small.

I believe that you could grant all I desire.

It's not enough!

He answers when I call;

My plans are so much more than you imagine.

So take my hand and follow where I lead.

What you ask is not too much;

It's far too small.

So I'll trust You

I'll trust Your love

I'll trust your plan for me.

By Debra G. Price

An Instrument of Praise

Make me an instrument of praise, O' Lord

Fill me with melodies of grace

Lift up my voice in song,

Proclaiming what is true

Make me an instrument

That's always praising you

By Debra G. Price

Here's My Life

Here It Is

Here it is, Lord;

I lay it on the altar;

A living sacrifice for you.

Fix my focus

And fill all my vision.

Create, in me, your own desires;

Here's my life.

Here are my feet;

Lead them in the right path.

Here are my hands;

Teach them how to serve.

Here is my voice;

Let it share your message.

Here is my heart;

Fill it with your love.

And when the world

Threatens to distract me,

Help me stand firm

Inside your will.

Here it is, Lord;

I lay it on the altar;

A living sacrifice for you.

Here's my life.

By Debra G. Price

Pain

It should be terminal;

The heart is broken.

Confidence is gone;

Fears felt, yet unspoken.

How can life continue?

More deeply felt is this

Than physical anguish,

Like death's own kiss.

From one who cared,

The poison dart

That sped on target

Straight to my heart.

The sacrifice completed,

Now he gloats,

Satisfied that he is well.

But Heaven notes:

For God knows.

Each broken aching part

Is carefully preserved

Next to His heart.

And life does go on;

With each day mending,

And strength returning

As God keeps sending

HOPE.

By Debra G. Price

He Speaks

In a still small voice

He will speak to you;

Giving you the choice

To freely do His will.

There are many voices speaking loud and long;

Crashing on your nerves like pounding waves.

And the urge to follow them is very strong;

Sweeping plans and purposes away.

Take the time to hear your gentle Shepherd's voice;

Searching through the brambles of your life.

Hear Him clearly , even in the loudest noise;

Calling you and list'ning for your cry.

Anywhere you go,

(If you stop to pray)

In your heart you'll know

He's whispering your name.

By Debra G. Price

Out of Bondage

The bondage of the body:

Bought and sold as slaves

To toil for another's gain.

Beaten down and forced to serve

A master moved by greed.

These chains could never bind:

A thought, a song, or a soul.

The bondage of the soul:

Born into slavery

To sin without thought or plan.

Trapped and tricked into serving

A master moved by hate.

These chains are broken by

A great sacrifice and simple faith.

The bondage of choice:

Volunteering as a bond slave

To work for another's glory.

Lifted up and blessed for serving

A Master moved by love.

Complete freedom from chains leading

To peace, joy, and Heaven.

By Debra G. Price

His Plan

God's plan for me may lead to other places;

To leave behind the things I understand.

How could I ever stay,

If He tells me when I pray:

To travel to a far and distant land.

The place I serve must be what He has chosen.

I'll walk the path that leads where He designs.

In God's pattern for today,

Any part that I would play,

Must be the role the Master has in mind.

For there's no peace outside the Savior's presence.

There is no safety without His guiding hand.

Real love and joy are known

Only where His fruit is grown.

My true home is found inside His perfect plan.

By Debra G. Price

If I Could

If I could hold a single snow flake

Unmelted in my hand,

Tracing the intricate design;

Still, I could not fully understand

The beauty of creation,

Or the treasure of salvation,

And how it can be mine.

If I could see through butterflies' wings

As though through crystal glass,

Discovering transparent hues;

Still, I could not glimpse what does surpass

The earthly realm I know,

Or the crown he will bestow,

And what of Heavenly views.

If I could climb upon a rainbow

Walking on the air,

With breath enough to sing and laugh;

Still, I could not find the strength to dare

The battle for one soul,

Or to reach a simple goal,

And walk the narrow path.

And yet, in Christ

Wisdom is free, Heaven is given,

Victory is certain.

By Debra G. Price

Courage

Don't be afraid

Your God is full of light;

And if you trust in Him

You can be sure

That things will turn out right.

He watches over you

All through the darkest night;

So don't forget,

You are always in His sight.

My little children

I hope you understand;

When the enemy

Surrounds you

God still holds you in His hand.

All through the battle

He is working out His plan.

Take courage children,

Step up and take your stand.

By Debra G. Price

The Music

My heart knows the music of Eternity.

It beats with the rhythm of a melody.

Sometimes in a minor key

It weeps for those who are lost.

Then in that marching beat

My vow is made at any cost

To take my life's music to a waiting world.

The Gospel's banner is my flag unfurled.

Now in a major strain

I'll sing though all alone;

Until the harmonies

Have reached to my Father's throne.

By Debra G. Price

Prayers

Sometimes my prayers seem wispy white;

They float on breezes of the night

Up where the galaxies are spinning through the sky.

The Spirit sifts them with great care

And sends them flying off somewhere,

Like perfumed incense drifting ever nigh.

While angels linger near the throne

The Father hears my prayer alone;

Each whispered word, each gentle thought, each heavy
sigh;

And though He takes the time to know

All these prayers like drifts of snow;

My slightest dreams are turned to answers by and by.

By Debra G. Price

Autumn's Festival

After the heat of summer

God sends the cool freshness of fall.

That's when His great festival begins.

He decorates with splashes of flaming colors;

He ripens the harvest to feed us with His unending bounty;

Then God laughs!

His laughter shakes the trees,

So they drop their golden leaves

Like confetti tossed on a breeze,

Whirling and twirling in a great joyous dance.

They become a carpet on the ground

That crackles under our feet,

Reminding us with every step

To be thankful

For God's festival

Called Autumn.

By Debra G. Price

Uncertain

Today life seems uncertain.

My future is not clear to me.

I struggle with my fears

And sometimes there are tears.

I long to feel security.

But God asks me to trust in

The love He has for me.

Although the path is dim,

I can walk this road with Him,

Becoming all that I could be;

And God is not uncertain,

He never feels confused or lost.

My tomorrows are as clear

The finish as secure

As if already past.

I can trust Him with my future,

He's perfecting His own plan,

And all I need tonight,

Is this moment's ray of light,

To reach out for His hand.

By Debra G Price

The Morning Waits

The Morning Waits

With charcoal black fingers forking upward

Wrapped in the frozen mist.

The morning waits.

I rise to meet her;

Stepping on the threshold of the winter's day.

Alone;

Yet He is there.

(His promises unfolding;

Of fresh snow, sun dazzled icicles, crisp air,

And care.)

Leading me onward through today;

To rest,

When night glows in winter white stillness;

For the morning waits

By Debra G. Price

www.ingramcontent.com/pod-product-compliance
Lightning Source LLC
Chambersburg PA
CBHW070112070426
42448CB00038B/2609